Relationship Networking 3.0

Building Relationships
and Getting Results
one person at a time

Terry Bass

Ordering information:

This book can be purchased online thru -

www.amazon.com

www.lulu.com

www.chadons.com

ISBN 978-0-557-07118-0

Table of Contents

Section I - Opening Thoughts
Chapter 1 - Introduction ..1
Chapter 2 - Defining Relationships ..5

Section II - Before You Network
Chapter 3 – Know Thyself ..9
Chapter 4 – Know Who's Coming ..13
Chapter 5 – Know Your Goals ..15
Chapter 6- Wrapping up this Section ..17

Section III- During
Chapter 7 –What will they see in the first 10 seconds? ..19
Chapter 8 – Some Do's & Don'ts ..21
Chapter 9 –- Your 30/60 Second Commercial ..23
Chapter 10 – Meeting New People ..27

SECTION IV – The Conversation
Chapter 11 – Body Language & Tone ..31
Chapter 12 - Getting Started ..33
Chapter 13 – The Conversation ..35

SECTION V – After
Chapter 14 – Keeping the Conversation Going ..39

Section VI - Uber-Networking
Chapter 15 –Mastering the Follow-Up ..41
Chapter 16 – Gaining Instant Credibility ..45

Section VII- Final Stuff
Chapter 17 - Closing Up ..49

Worksheet ..51
About the Author ..53

Chapter 1

Introduction

It is generally acknowledged that people should be doing two things no matter their status. It doesn't matter whether you are working or not working. Manager or stay at home parent. New to the business world or retired. And so on. Those two things are -

- Personal/Professional Development
- Networking

Personal/Professional Development keeps us moving forward. Our skills and experiences constantly growing. Studies show that not only is this important mentally, but by showing a constant willingness and desire to learn new things and expand our knowledge, we create positive impressions, impressing others (like our boss or prospective boss!).

The second thing is of course Networking. What this book is about.
Networking essentially increases possibilities. That sounds kind of lame, but the fact is, what YOU are looking for will be different than others, however, it really doesn't matter. The fact is that whether you are looking for more leads, clients, a mentor, a job, resources for your business, work or personal life, just a new friend, or anything else, by networking you *increase the possibilities* of that happening. IF you sit on your butt at home, you don't.
And the statistics support that. Approximately 70% of all jobs are found through some type of networking. Around 80% of all business sales are found through the same way.

And where you see them looking for business, building relationships and just meeting people is your local networking events. There are tons of people out there networking hoping to increase their possibilities.

The problem arises that very few people know the true value of networking and how to network effectively. Many either fumble through and don't create much of a first impression or you'll see people come and basically socialize. So what is it that you can do to make your time more worthwhile?

Welcome to Relationship Networking 3.0.

While there are a gazillion books on networking, they basically fall into two schools.

The first school is the "**hunter**" school and it's based primarily on getting clients. The hunter will have very specific sales goals, focusing very quickly on whether the person they are talking to can be a potential client, quickly setting up the next meet to close the deal and then shifting on to the next person. If the person is not seen as a potential client, the hunter quickly moves on.

My experience is that there are very, very few people that can do this successfully. People that act like a hunter tend to be pretty obvious and create negative impressions, resulting in a success rate of close to zero. And so what you see is the seond school of networking.

The second is the "building relationship" school or being a "**farmer**" instead of a hunter. This is where you plant the seeds to grow potential relationships and see what happens. The expected results are building a long term, mutually profitable relationship.

The challenge for farmers is that where does the socializing end and the "business" begin? Are you going to networking events, chatting away with mostly people you know and then calling it a night? Are you really accomplishing anything?

This book attempts to take a middle ground, a hybrid of the two schools, taking the best aspects of each. Let's introduce the "**explorer**" school.

The explorer is curious, dives into the unknown, creating and building relationships, yet wants to get some kind of results. The explorer will see where the results take them.
And so it should be for you when you network.

As a non-stop networker, I am a strong believer in meeting lots of people and creating relationships with as many people as I can. Are the people I'm meeting going to buy my services? Maybe. Maybe not. But they also could be people who's services I could use.   Or somebody I know could use their services.

They could be people who are connected with someone else, or an association/organization that I have an interest in. They could just be somebody that is in an industry that could be of interest to me, personally or professionally. Won't know until I meet them and discover the possibilities! They could also turn into a friend, mentor, some form of resource or help me get a job someplace. There are all sorts of potential!

The simple fact in life is that the more people you know, the better placed you will be no matter where your future takes you. I haven't heard of anyone who has ever suffered from knowing too many people!

However, when I network, I don't want to just meet people and leave it at that. After all I could be home with reading a good book, in my sweats drinking a cold beer. So lets try and create some useful results for our effort.

That's where we take the opportunity to meet someone new and explore the possibilities of a relationship. The best relationships are those that benefit each other. It's not necessary to be searching for more personal friends, you probably have enough of those. However, you never, ever will have enough business friends!

So welcome to the explorer school of networking, where we will focus on meeting people, creating various types of quality relationships (not just vendor/client), and do a little goal setting and focusing, so that the time you spend networking can be more productive for you, your career and your business.

The bottom line when networking, is that you want people to come away with two things - a positive impression of you and the possibility of creating and building a jointly beneficial relationship. This book is loaded with tips on how to do just that.

Lastly, I'm suppose to tell you that I'm the only one responsible for what you're going to be reading. So there you have it.

Let's get started.

Chapter 2

Defining Relationships

Let's first define Relationships.

Relationships are built by 3 basic elements. As the image to the right shows, they are -
- Like
- Trust
- Respect

But all things are not equal either. In any relationship, we will Like, Trust and Respect different people, different amounts. We could for example have a high maintenance friend who is fun to go out with (high Like!), but frankly we think their lives are a train wreck and we know we really can't count on them for much (low Trust and Respect).

Or how about the colleague that we don't have much in common with or don't know very well personally, but is a great co-worker that you can always count on (low Like, higher Trust/Respect) and so on.

We could know a person that we don't normally Respect, but we DO know that if they say they are going to do something, we can Trust that they will carry it out.
Like, Trust, Respect.

Some thoughts on Like, Trust and Respect.
The opposite of Like is not that you dislike the person. You just may feel you don't have anything in common with them.
Trust and Respect may appear to be the same, yet they're not. Respect is built on the past or present. You have seen them in action and you respect their work, ethics, etc. Trust is based on the future. If you give them some work or a referral, you Trust that they will take care of it professionally. Somewhat linked, but still different.

The combination of Like, Trust and Respect will give us an idea of the quality of the relationship and what you can expect from it.

Which brings us to our LTR Meter (Like, Trust, Respect). We have virtual LTR Meter's for every one we meet. People will start out low and as we get to know them better, our Like, Trust and Respect will grow and the arrow moves up on the meter.

Or maybe not. There certainly could be people that we meet or know, that we don't have much Like/Trust/Respect for, so it stays starts low and stays low, which is a pretty good indication that we don't have much of a relationship!

This is important to understand as we network.
Let's meet someone. At this point, we're pretty low on the LTR Meter. We might get a modicum of Like/Trust/Respect, but it's not likely to grow much in one conversation. At the end, we exchange business cards and never follow up. We put the business cards in our database system and that's as far as it goes.

Have we built much of a relationship? Not really. The chances of the individual even remembering you after some time lapse is pretty slim. So what did you achieve with the time and effort you just spent?

What do you <u>want</u> to achieve?

If we are looking at the sales angle and looking at people as potential clients, we want one (or more) of three possible results.

1.We want them to become our customer now.
2.If not now, we want them to remember us for when they could use our product/services sometime in the future.
3.If they have no need of our product/services now or in the future, we would love for them to refer us to THEIR network of friends, family and associates. This is the golden egg for ANY business!

However, if all we had is a quick conversation (barely moving the LTR Meter), what is the chance of any of the above happening?
It's a well know axiom, that people have to first buy you, then your company, and THEN your product/services. Building relationships, understanding and moving that LTR meter helps you to do exactly that!

The same applies to someone who has the potential of becoming a mentor, gateway, guide, resource or even friend. If you take the time and effort needed to build your relationship by increasing your Like/Trust/Respect, the higher that LTR meter points, the greater likelihood you'll have of gaining more from that relationship.

So how do you build that Like/Trust/Respect?
Lots of ways. But frequency of contact, taking the time of getting to know the person, as well as shared interests builds relationships.
I'm sure you've also heard the term "giver's gain". Giving and helping someone out whether through referrals, guidance, or even just a cool book you've read or website you've visited will certainly increase their Like/Trust/Respect of you.

You will be receiving lots of tips throughout this book on how to build and sustain your relationships.

Also understand that there is the likelihood of a difference in your LTR Meter and theirs. One of you can certainly Like/Trust/Respect the other at a higher level than the other. And that's ok.

For example, I am a speaker and even give short talks at networking events. This raises my visibility and credibility with the other people listening (hopefully!). After watching me (or any other good speaker for that matter) it only makes sense that people will have a higher Like, Trust, Respect for the speaker, then the speaker will for them only because I haven't even had the opportunity to meet them yet.

When you network, you meet dozens, if not hundreds of people. The fact is, not much is likely to happen with the vast majority of them. They don't know you and you don't know them. No relationship. However the people that you do take the time and effort to grow that Like, Trust and Respect with, building a relationship, the greater likelihood of them wanting to do business with you.

Chapter 3

Know Thyself

There are a couple things you should know about yourself in regards to networking.

It helps to know if are you an extrovert or introvert. There are a few personality evaluations that deal with this like Myers-Briggs or I Disc (both of which can be found and taken on the internet for about 50 bucks).

This is important to know because extroverts and introverts deal with networking differently. Common myths are that it's better to be an extrovert to network, while introverts will have a hard time being successful. That's absolutely untrue. Both extro's and intro's have their own strengths for networking and their own weaknesses. The intelligent networker first understands where they are on the scale of extrovert and introvert and uses the strengths (and works on the weaknesses) to their advantage.

Next myth. Introverts are uncomfortable meeting strangers. The fact is EVERYONE is uncomfortable meeting strangers. And that's ok. Understanding that a major part of networking will be meeting new people, we just need to be aware that being an extrovert or introvert has nothing to do with it.

For years (much to the amusement of virtually everyone that knew me) I considered myself an introvert since I was not comfortable going up to perfect strangers. I have gone through several "personality profiles" and the one consistent thing is that I am pegged as a strong extrovert. So I better understand myself now along with what I need to work on to be more successful; which was learning to meet new people just like everybody else!

What are the 2 big differences when networking for extroverts and introverts?

- The <u>way</u> we are comfortable interacting with other people
- Our Personal Energy (not the new-agey stuff, read on)

OK it is true, extroverts love to interact in groups. If you're networking and see a group of 4 or 5 people (or more) with one person "holding court", chances are you're seeing an extrovert in action. Extroverts are bigger, more expansive, the hand gestures will be more pronounced!

The challenge for extroverts is that many of us do love to talk. Extroverts can be fun, hold a group together, provide energy, but they also are likely to do most of the talking. You will learn about the extrovert all sorts of things, but they may not learn much about you. Not necessarily good for building relationships.

So if this is you as an extrovert, you need to learn to scale back, give others the chance to talk and get involved in the discussion, learn about other people.

The introvert is not someone who has difficulty networking. They just have to do it a little differently.

Introverts are more comfortable typically one on one. Two people talking to each other is the perfect networking environment for anyone and that happens to be the comfort zone for intro's . Introverts are more likely cede talking time than others, but might still need to learn how to listen properly (just like everyone else).

Quick Tip - For an introvert, groups are probably not going to be a comfortable environment, so if there is someone in a group that you want to talk to, separate them from the herd! Take them aside and create that one on one space that you are apt to be more comfortable in.

10

As mentioned, the other differentiator between extro's and intro's can be energy levels.

Think of a long day at work. You're tired, but you have to go to some networking event. Geesh!

The extrovert on one hand, while maybe starting out tired, starts getting energized as the networking event progresses. Extroverts basically get energy from groups and gatherings. Extroverts can typically last the night away!

Heck, as the event draws to a close, the extrovert might even try to get a group together and head out for a beer!

Understand that the extrovert will probably crash on the way home. They no longer have the group feeding them that energy and on the car ride home, tiredness will set back in. That's ok. The extrovert just needs to watch themselves because they may have a huge energy drop as the event winds down.

The introvert on the other hand essentially loses energy at group events. And if there was a long, tough day at work, the last thing you want to do is go networking.

So it's important for an intro' to recharge first.

Perhaps between work and networking, stop someplace, do a caffeine and sugar thing, maybe if alone time with a book helps you recharge, stop at Starbucks or Mickey D's and take a half hour by yourself.

Quick Tip - How about stopping at your favorite store like Best Buy or clothing or outdoor store? Roam the aisles, fantasize about your next vacation, that humongous screen TV. Figure out whatever works for get you re-energized and focused on the networking event ahead and take a breather.

11

If you show up a little late that's fine, especially if you are now more ready to dive in!

Quick Tip – This applies to the extro's also. If you had a rough day at work, head out for a little diversion and get the mind clear. Nothing is worse than being someplace that you don't want to be. And trust me, it shows!

Lastly, the introvert needs to understand that you may not last the whole time. Figure out what you can handle. Don't make this an excuse to leave early (or not attend at all!) but try different things that will help you be on top of your game when you do network. It could be a more productive time for you by being "all there" for 2 hours of a 3 hour event, then physically there, but mentally in la-la land for that 3rd hour.

It's to your advantage to understand where you sit on the extrovert/introvert scale and what are your strength's and possible challenges are when networking. This way, you can adjust your schedule or behavior to maximize your networking, making it more successful and enjoyable for you.

The bottom line is that if networking is an arduous chore for you, it doesn't matter what you are trying to accomplish. You won't be enjoying the time spent meeting new people, chances are you'll be less productive or effective and it will show.

Chapter 4

Know Who's Coming

Many networking events now register on-line and list who is attending along with their company.
Even if you registered early, a lot of people wait until the last minute, so the best time to check out who's coming is a couple hours prior.
OK, so now you know who's showing up, now what?

Is there anybody that you would like to meet on that list? It doesn't even have to be someone that you would like to sell to. This is where you start thinking outside the box. (I know, I know, old cliché, but it really fits here!)

For example, your business has printers (don't they all) and a guy from a discount cartridge place is going to be there. Would he be a good person to talk to in maybe helping you reduce costs? Even if you are an employee. What would happen if you turned your boss on to a way to save money for your organization? Wouldn't you look good?

How about that lawyer, real estate agent, chiropractor? Is their some information that they might have to help you personally or professionally? Maybe you want to find out where the lawyer's congregate, or what associations in the area they belong to (for you to better market yourself). How about some dirt on the condos going up next to your office?

The point I am attempting to make is that there is a wealth of information, ideas and experience that will be at any networking event. To focus strictly on people being prospective buyers severely limits the benefits you can get from meeting new people.
Chances are the things that are challenging you right now (how to market, where to market, next steps, getting more clients, etc.) someone may have an answer or at least a direction that could help you and your business.

How about personally, maybe not even for yourself? Is there someone going to be there that can help you get an answer for a friend or family member?

Is there some industry that you might be interested in, whether just interested in or possibly as a career change? Will somebody be there that you find out more about that industry, the pitfalls? Who knows, your next employer could be there!

Quick tip – You can chose to look at people as potential clients or you can choose to look at people as possible resources for your whole life spectrum. Those that network with this expanded outlook reap greater gains.

Also by checking out who is coming and marking down a few people that you might want to talk to gets you circulating when you arrive.
Having some specific people that you want to meet, you will move around, check out name tags and introducing yourself. A great way to get you in action.

By looking beyond the "possible client" and pursuing other opportunities to get to know your networking contacts (and what they know), you open the door to creating deeper relationships, finding solutions for your business/career and making your networking time much more effective and enjoyable.

Quick Tip – What if your network coordinator doesn't post who's attending? ASK! Call and see if they have a list made up (they should have it on some excel spreadsheet). Chances are they'll be more than happy to email it to you for your perusal. And you'll be ahead of everyone else at the event!
Don't ask for email addresses (they probably won't hand them out), just their name and company so that you can determine who you may want to talk to.

14

Chapter 5

Know Your Goals

Certainly adopting the previous chapter idea would be a great start to making a goal for networking. But there are certainly other goals that you can focus on as well depending on what you want to accomplish. Some of those could be...

- Planning on getting an X appointments to follow up.
- Plan on getting to know someone better (building that relationship), maybe someone you met previously.
- Getting a certain amount of business cards.
- Finding someone more experienced in the business than you, and see if you can have them mentor you a bit or just sit and talk with you, sharing experience and pitfalls.
- Finding someone from a less mainstream industry or just one you're not familiar with and see if it could be a market of interest to you and discover where THEY meet.
- Meet someone that could "partner" with you, someone that may have a different business, but similar clients. Could you do something (advertise, host an event) that would bring in both sets of clients and maybe help each other.
- Introducing yourself to the hosts (if a chamber event, the officers and the people who work at the chamber).
- Plan on meeting X amount of **new** people (an essential and great networking goal!).
- _____ (create your own goal that makes sense for you and your business!

Making goals doesn't have turn into this high pressure "business" thing. But BY making goals, you are more likely avoid what the vast majority of networkers do, which is to show up, talk to some people (often people they already know) and then head home. You also get a better sense of satisfaction at the end of the day, when you achieved those goals!

Quick Tip – Write your goals down, put it on a spreadsheet with the events you go to. Keep track of what goals you achieve and where. If you're not achieving those goals, figure out why.
Is it because you're not doing the right things, or is it because maybe you're not going to the right networking event?

Sometimes you might WANT to just hang out with people you know after a long day. That's ok.
Plan on spending the first half meeting new people, etc. and then spending the second half relaxing with your friends.

At the end of the day, networking is taking time away from other things that you can be doing. By having some goals, you'll feel better about the time spent and be able to see real results at the same time.

Chapter 6

Wrapping Up This Section

Successful people in any business today know the value of preparation. For some meetings, the preparation can take a great deal longer than the meeting itself. But good prep is likely to create good meetings. It is no different with networking.

The good news is preparation time for networking is pretty short, checking out where your head is at (Know ThySelf), the prospective attendees (Know Who's Coming), and what you want to accomplish (Know Your Goals). In fact, after doing it a time or two, it will be pretty natural and take just a few minutes. But like any preparation, payoff is significant.

You can expect to have more meaningful networking events. You will open yourself up to learning more, getting to know more people, having more people know you, building better, stronger relationships, opening yourself up to opportunities that you may not have considered before.

Making networking a more profitable experience for you.

Chapter 7

What Will they See In the First 10 Seconds?

Several studies show that people make their first impression within 5 – 15 seconds of seeing you. What you are wearing, how you are standing, your whole body language. All sorts of things before they even may begin talking with you. It makes sense that if you want to build professional relationships, you will want to remove any obstacles to creating that positive first impression.

What is the image you wish to project? Do you want to say that you are a professional, for you and your company to be taken seriously? Then if what you're wearing is more appropriate for social than business networking, maybe you need to rethink your outfit. Sometimes throwing on a jacket can do the trick and look more professional.

Quick Tip - If you are a business owner of an industry that allows a more casual look, polo shirts with a company name/logo look great and can be gotten for a reasonable price (even if only purchasing a couple).

Sometimes not only looking professional, but acting professional can be a challenge especially towards the end of the day, but you need to remember that you ARE projecting an image of you and your organization.

You don't have to be serious or so wrapped up in not making any gaffes or mistakes that you are uncomfortable. Finding that right balance of being you, yet a professional will always steer you in the right direction.

Chapter 8

Some Do's & Don'ts

• **Have a name tag that is legible and can be seen.**
People are more comfortable approaching someone where they can clearly see their name and company. It can start the conversation and makes it easier to remember the important stuff like who you are and who you represent! Textbook says to put the tag on your right side, so that as you shake hands, its visible to the other person.

Quick Tip – Make your own name tag. Get one of those "show badges" that hang around your neck, print out a card that has your name in big, easy to read type, your company name and a point you want to make (website, slogan, logo) Make a knot in the back so that it sits on your chest (and not at navel height) so people can easily read it. Your own badge then shows you're a pro, is easier to read and you can stick a few business cards in the back for easy exchange when the time comes!

• **Always have business cards.**
Business cards don't sell you or your business, but they do help people to remember you and what you do and give people that essential contact information. A good rule of thumb – ANYTIME you leave your house, you should have up to date business cards in your hand.

Quick Tip – To ensure that you don't show up with no cards, take a healthy chunk of them from the box, put them in a baggie and place them in the center console or glove box of your car. This way, if you forget them or run low, they are handy to restock.

• **Shake hands firmly.**
One of the common mistakes people make is to shake hands limply when shaking hands especially with women. Don't be a bone crusher, but a hand shake should be firm no matter your gender or the recipients. It expresses confidence.

• **Go over to the person standing alone and introduce yourself.**
Always strive to meet new people.
First because they are available to talk, and also because
chances are they'd be grateful in having someone "break the
ice" (and isn't that making a great first impression?) If you chat
with them and know someone they should know, connect the
two. This IS what networking is all about, and you now have
two people thinking good thoughts about you!

• **Don't just talk to people you know.**
That's the whole idea of networking. Meeting new people. If
you've been to the same group, as one of your goals make a
personal commitment (that's goal) to meet a certain amount
of new people each time or maybe get to know others better.
Let's face it, if you're just talking to people you already know,
you're socializing, not networking. And is that really what you
want to accomplish then and there?
Quick tip – If you do want to talk to your friends, commit to
"networking" the first half and then relax with your pals the
second half. Or grab a friend and network together! Then you
can compare notes later.

• **Don't hand out flyers.**
You're trying to build relationships. Flyers give you the excuse
to not talk and people generally don't like them at networking
events since then THEY have to then carry them around, etc.
An exception could be when you are offering a discount or
deal". Even then it might make sense to leave it on a table
near the door.

• **Thank people on your way out.**
Courtesy never steers you wrong. If the event is held at a
business, thank the host. Don't forget to thank the organizer's
or if there is a sponsor. Just a quick "thanks, great event" will
suffice. It may lead to conversation or not, but you are showing
people you appreciate their efforts and that only makes them
think positively about you.

Chapter 9

Your 30/60 Second Commercial

The 30/60 second commercial will be when you introduce yourself to an individual or a group.

When you introduce yourself, **your purpose is to pique interest so that they will have a desire to have a discussion with you.**

Many people when they network, recite a menu of their services during their commercial. Unfortunately what that does is put the listener in the position of thinking (perhaps falsely).."ok, I have a good idea of what they offer and I have no need for their services". Yet there is a good chance that you in fact didn't tell them everything that you do or provide, however the conversation is over before it had a chance to begin.

Another challenge during the commercial can be your job title. Does that create a strong image of what you do? "I'm a realtor" will pretty much define you and the listener will automatically be determining if they really want to talk with you. What if the realtor instead introduced themselves by saying, "I help people get maximum value out of their home when they are buying or selling." Would that be more likely to pique your interest?
Part of the reason I use business coach as my job title is that it is recognized, but not clearly understood what a business coach does. People aren't sure exactly what that means, so they are likely to start a conversation to better understand my services more. Exactly what I want!

So how can you define yourself that will generate interest?

However you do it, you have a few brief seconds to grab someone's interest. You'll know you succeeded when people think or say "oh really? Tell me more!"

It's always important to have a good idea of what you would like to say in whatever time you are given.

Have a few different ways of introducing yourself. Don't always say the same thing. Can you rephrase your basic message? Unfortunately, what usually happens when you continually give the same spiel, is that YOU sound bored and rote, rattling off your lines. Not a good way to capture peoples interest.

Quick Tip: The good networker always respects the time given. Taking advantage and babbling on (and on) about everything you offer with your business is a turn off and frankly makes you look silly.

Let's say you are given the opportunity to introduce yourself to the group at large - to give that 30 or 60 second commercial. What should you say?

First think 30 seconds.
Certainly provide you're name & company. **And then the hook.** An effective hook is something that will interest people and want them to talk to you after the introductions.

Can you mention what you do in such a way that intrigues people? But you need to do it honestly. If the hook is "I have a program that can save every business lots of money", is it true and something they won't feel conned (for showing interest) when they hear the solution? The hook shouldn't be mysterious, just interesting.

It doesn't even have to be business related!
For a long time I threw out that I recently had Lasik surgery. People would then come over to me and ask me how it went, etc. and we would have a conversation creating rapport and eventually getting around to business.

I then gave them Lasik tips, offered to email them info on where I went, hand them coupons that I was given. All steps to creating that relationship. It gave me the opportunity to contact them again to see if they did the eye surgery. No sales push, just continuing to build that common ground.
NOTE: I brought my Lasik into the commercial by talking about how a business coach can help you improve yourself, accept change, try new things. An example of change is that I just got Lasik surgery and its changed my life dramatically. I'd usually close with doing a witty - Don't worry I'm not offering to operate a laser on your eyes, but I can help dramatically improve or change your business!
People would then come over to me and I had the opportunity to continue all sorts of conversation.

Another great hook I had was when I mentioned that I was subpoenaed recently. That had EVERYONE listening. I then would mention how I was a witness to a car/bicycle collision. I tied it together by mentioning the dangers of not keeping your eyes on the road ahead and that's what a business coach can help with. Unorthodox sure, but it grabbed attention and bunches of people would then come up and chat with me.

The next step is to have the flexibility to expand your commercial to 60 seconds!

At 60 seconds, you will use much of what you say in the 30 and add something new.

The best thing to offer is testimonials - "People who have used my services see a savings, increase in business of XXX".
Or being a problem solver - "Businesses today have a tough time in this market being different from the rest and our role is to make your business really different and unique by...." Or "many companies are fighting the high cost of XXX and a simple no cost revue by our people has saved significant money for 2 out of 3 businesses that we meet."

These are just a couple of examples of being a solution provider or problem solver.

People may want to talk about a new feature that is exciting to them. The range of services may be a unique point that they are excited about, however it could be that the ordinary layman doesn't understand and probably doesn't care! You see that often with financial advisors and bankers. They get all a twitter over a new interest rate, that's A QUARTER POINT OVER THE COMPETITION! <snore> Does it generate interest with the audience you are in front of? If not, why mention it?

And practice, practice, practice. So that it's smooth, no ah's and um's, and generally around the time frame (30-60 seconds) given.
- If you network frequently or with a networking group, try out different approaches and see how they react.
- Use humor or current events, anything that can tie in what you do and how you can help them.
- Be real and be interesting and
- don't read the menu!

People may already have the same product/services from someone else. They may not. When you network, what you're selling is YOU! So quit focusing so much at the introductory stage on the product/services and instead market YOU.

Remember the idea you want in their head when you have completed your commercial isn't "I understand what that person does", but "hmm, maybe they are someone that can help me, I should meet them and find out more".

Chapter 10

Meeting New People

First myth.
Only some people (namely you) are uncomfortable meeting strangers. The fact is EVERYONE starts out with some degree of discomfort in walking up and introducing themselves to perfect strangers. We can probably blame our parents for this one too. (Always a convenient trick).
We have been taught from the cradle to "not talk to strangers" for a very good safety reason. But it HAS carried into our adult lives and it really doesn't matter what the occasion, the vast majority of us really have a difficult time walking up and meeting someone we don't know.

This happens certainly in social occasions. Have you ever been to a party where there are several groups of people? You know, work friends, neighborhood friends and maybe sports club friends. And pretty much during the course of the party they remain in their 3 distinct groups, each eyeing the other seeing if there is someone interesting, seeing if they should or can "cross the line". Really kind of silly, isn't it?
Similar things happen at business networking events. You see the newbie's (that don't know anyone) standing up against the wall, drink in hand, looking like a deer in the headlights. Then there's the "old hands" grouped together chatting away with old comrades they obviously know. And there are a few brave souls circulating around the room.

So how do you meet new people?
The solution. Just do it. Honestly, it really is the trick.

Try an experiment. Go up to someone that you don't know (you can do this anywhere) and greet them. Do they bite your head off, snarl, run to the bathroom and wash their hands, give you a disgusted look? NO! Of course they don't.

In fact, especially if they were standing around and not interacting with someone, they're certainly going to be appreciative
that someone joined them.
Next step is to do that whole networking thing. Get to know
them, ask them questions about themselves and so on. Good
chances you'll meet an interesting person with some common
bonds to build a relationship with.

Think about it. You wouldn't have met them if you didn't just
bite the bullet and go up to them. So now that you did,
hopefully you had a good conversation, met an interesting
person, maybe have something in common. Now what?
Repeat.
**Meeting new people should be enjoyable, not some scary
hurdle to overcome.**

Part of peoples nervousness is that you are putting yourself
out there, that you are representing yourself, your company
and your product. Possible rejection, lack of interest,
dismissal.

*The fact of the matter is networking isn't about selling; it's
about creating and building relationships. So take a deep
breath and remember that the first time you meet someone,
you shouldn't be "selling" or "prospecting", you should just be
getting to know them, build a rapport and find out what they
do and so on.*

And the biggest, coolest trick in the book is...Ask.
Ask them what they do. Ask them where they live.
Ask them how they like their job. Ask them what interests
them.
Ask them to clarify something when you don't understand.
Just Ask.

People love to talk about themselves especially if you show an
interest. So, ask away! You're not on the hook. You're not on

the spot to "produce answers", you get the chance to know someone and the conversation will flow pretty naturally.

And there will be a conversation. At some point they will ask about you, so yes, you still have to have an elevator speech about yourself and what you do. And who knows, as mentioned before, you may find a common interest, even a reason to do business together. **But the primary focus when you first meet someone is to introduce yourself and get to know them.**

Whew! Sound a bit easier now?
As I've mentioned earlier, I happen to be a strong extrovert; I'm a really outgoing guy. But even I had a tough time learning this and still sometimes have trouble today going to an event and just getting started!

When I see the person standing alone, it's something that I CAN do to help in a small way. I walk over, introduce myself and ask what they do. And off the conversation goes.
I have met a lot of great people that way!

Many times, I've been able to take the newbie and introduce them to someone else, someone with a common interest. That's networking and that's life. In retrospect, one of the great things about my work is meeting a range of people with a wide range of careers and experiences that I would never have known about. It encourages me to know more. And what a great place to be.

So go ahead, say hi.
Introduce yourself and ASK.
It'll be more fun and a great use of your time.
And who knows, the next person you meet could end up being a colleague, a gateway to your next job, a client, a drinking buddy, a friend.
And it starts with you walking up to them and say hello.

Chapter 11

Body Language & Tone

When we talk, we actually communicate 3 ways.

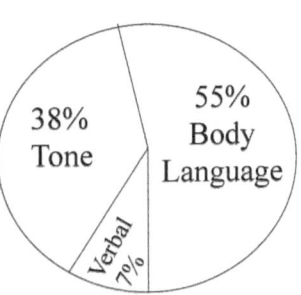

The first is verbal, the words we say. The second is the tone of our voice. The third is our body language.

Our words are only 7% of how people register what we are telling them (especially the more stressed or emotional we are at the time). People are actually picking up (albeit maybe sub-consciously) much more from our Tone and Body Language, that other 93%!

A good example of this is listening to someone that you think is not being honest with you. They are saying the right words, but you still think they are attempting to pull one over on you. You are certainly picking up something in their tone of voice or body language that is not in agreement with what they are saying.

Are you saying the right words, but are sounding bored? Is your body language letting the person know that you really aren't listening to them or they aren't that important? *Have you ever talked to someone that is constantly looking around? Their body language is practically screaming at you that you're not that important. Is that the impression you would want to give?* Guess what? People sense that. They may not know why, but they are picking up the signal. So be aware of that.

Understand that you or they may just be tired. However by being aware of how tone and body language can influence your communications with other people gives you a better chance of getting the right message across!

Quick Tip –

You have two people directly facing each other,
This is the "closed position. It can be difficult to
"break in" this type of conversation. If there is someone that
you really want to talk to, either come back later when they've
"opened up" or stand to the side patiently until someone ac-
knowledges you. (always apologize for interrupting them)

Then there is the "open triangle". That means
while they are talking, they are open to other
people joining them. You can then come in and
"close" the triangle, introducing yourself when they
look your way.

YOU

Don't forget to make eye contact with who you are having the conversation with. People who don't make eye contact are thought to be unsure of themselves or dishonest or even just bored. Not the impression you want people to have of you.

These are a couple of things to think about around body language as well as tone. Understand the need to be conscious of the signals you are giving or getting from people as you network. The more cognizant you are of what people are telling you by not only what they say, but through their tone of voice and body language, the better you can respond and communicate more effectively.

Chapter 12

Getting Started

In Do's and Don'ts, I wrote about meeting people that are standing alone and how they can be great people to meet. It's easy. You just walk over and say hello. Never a bad thing. Or do you want to join a conversation already in play, what now?

A reminder that the important difference between networking and socializing is when you are networking you are meeting new people or people that you would like to know better, that creating and building relationships stuff. When you're socializing, you're just chatting with the same old crowd. And (again) is that an effective use of your time?

So now you're standing in front of someone, shook hands (firmly) and are making eye contact, where do you start?

Although a lot of networking books tell people not to say "So what do you do?" almost everybody does, or something similar. I personally don't have a problem with it, after all, the whole idea of networking is to meet people and find out what they do! If you want change it around a bit, "So what brings you here?"

Make sure you have a good "elevator speech" about what you do and good follow up. It should be succinct, interesting and you know you succeeded when the person says, "tell me more"? People often focus on the initial statement and ignore having a good follow up. What often happens is that you lose focus and could start babbling or reading that menu! Keeping people interested in you is what you want to do.

Quick Tip – You find yourself babbling, people's eyes glazing over or looking around, how do you get out of that?
..You can say, "So enough about me, tell me (more of) what you do".

Chapter 13

The Conversation

Now that we have some basics down, let's break the Conversation into two parts, Listening and then Talking, two different skills.

Listening is often misunderstood. Most people think of listening as "not talking". We think we are doing pretty good if we don't interrupt. That's a start, but only the start.
So can you listen, really listen and not just "not talk"? People often let other people talk, but then spend their time thinking about what they are going to say next, thinking about their favorite sports team or a show they are missing right now.

Listening is really focusing on what the person is saying. In the book *"What Got You Here Won't Get You There"* by Marshall Goldsmith, he talks about it as **listening with respect.** We all have people that we love talking to because they happen to be listening with respect. You get the sense that right there, right then, you are the most important person to them. When that happens, how does that make you feel? Would you like people to be thinking of YOU the same way? Just listen with respect.

Think about a first date, professionally or personally, someone you are trying to impress. You hang on their every word, you are attentive to what they say and even focus enough to pick up what they aren't saying. You feel connected with that person as they talk, you are bonding. You can do it, you just need to learn to do it regularly.
Why? As mentioned before, the other person is picking up that you are really interested in them and responds well to that. It creates a great positive impression about you.

Quick Tip – A good measure of how much you should not be talking (therefore listening!) is equal to the quantity of people.

If there are two of you, then you should be listening at least ½ the time, three of you, 1/3 of the time and so on. This way you are not dominating the conversation and give the others the chance to talk about themselves.

Ok, so you've shown you're a good listener and now is the chance to talk. This is an excellent opportunity to really screw it up when you open your mouth to speak!

In seminar after seminar, this is what people tell me is their greatest fear....what do I say?

Certainly being in tune with what the conversations likely to be helps. Is this a geographically based event? (ie: chamber) Subscribe to the local newspaper and read about local happenings. How about industry focused groups like associations? Get their magazines or newsletters. You don't have to be an expert blabbing out your opinion to everyone you meet (and in fact that might NOT be a good idea!), but even if you're just listening to the conversation your body language will show that you're tracking the conversation and conversant with what's going on.

This shows you as part of the group, an insider. I regularly network in areas not my own. I COULD be seen as an outsider, however by having an awareness of the issues of the area that I'm in, a potential negative gets neutralized and often impresses people that I'm aware of what's going on even though I don't live in the area and interested enough to pay attention to the local goings on.

Even with that, the best words out of a persons mouth are questions or openings for people to talk about themselves.

"Tell me about yourself..your company..your industry".

"What kind of customers do you like?"

"How do you do that?" And so on.

People love to talk about themselves and what they do. When you ask questions, you have the ability to gather information about them and their organization as well as showing yourself to be someone interested in their life, creating a great impression.

But you ARE going to get the opportunity to talk and you should....

• be enthusiastic about what you do and what you are doing now. Keep your energy and enthusiasm up. If you mumble or by your tone of voice don't sound too thrilled about what your doing, *why would someone want to do business with you*? But being enthusiastic doesn't mean you go on...and on...and on.

• be aware of using fillers – ummm/s or "like" or "and stuff". It's filler. It means that you don't know what you are saying. It's distracting from the message you wish to give.

• never whine about work or you're busy day. Again, why would people want to do business with someone that doesn't like their job? I have met several people who will rant about how screwed up their boss and/or company is. I understand the bad day at the office, however in a professional setting, you're wasting my time and definitely not creating a good Impression of you or your business.

• not inundate people with everything that you do. Some people have a lot of offerings (that menu again)....who cares? The purpose of networking is to form relationships. Even if they are a potential new customer, the purpose usually is to get a meeting. If you are pushing your product, you're selling, and nobody is interested. Stay focused, always keeping an eye on what you want to achieve.

QUICK TIP - want to remember names?

After they introduce themselves, try and repeat it at appropriate times at least 3 times –

Shaking hands – "well, nice meeting jack.", "So tell me Susan, what is it that you do?", "It was great talking to you Paul....." or when taking the business card, read it and comment "Julie, what a great logo..your office is in?..anything to use the name and not just stuffing the business card in your pocket.

A good conversation will range over business, personal, sports and local happenings. As mentioned before, it benefits you to be prepared and read news so that you can converse or at least understand what people are talking about. You don't need to be a sports fan to pass over the sports pages and know the major players, who is being traded and so on. Having said that, don't pass yourself off as an expert if you're not. Just nod and let the others do the talking. They'll be more than happy to.

Quick tip – you now want to leave a conversation tactfully, but not sure how? Remember the body language section with the diagrams of the two people talking? Move your body from any closed position into the "open triangle" position relative to your partner leaving an opening for someone to come in. At their arrival, get them to start conversing and then excuse yourself.

Anybody can talk. The networker's goal is to create a positive impression. Being conversant and yet letting someone else do the talking is a great way to create the impression you want.

So learn to listen and let them do the talking. You'll learn more about them and their business. And even though you may not have said much, there's a pretty good chance at the end of the conversation, they'll shake your hand and say "Hey it was great talking with you!"

Chapter 14

Keeping the Conversation Going

You're done. The networking event is over. You did everything Terry told you to do (well most) and whew, you can now relax. Not quite yet.

You now have met some people and maybe got an appointment or agreement to meet. So now what? Obviously, the people that you are going to meet get attention. As soon as possible, contact them for a concrete date and time if you haven't already done so.

Networking is to gain favorable attention. Post-Networking should be focused on keeping your name, company and services in front of the potential client.
So write a handwritten note about how nice it was to meet them. Very few people do that and if you do, it will make you more memorable.

Quick Tip – Have stationary that has your business name, contact information, website on it. That way, "the nice meeting you" note is sincere, and not loaded with your business card but you still have the information if they wish to contact you and find out more about you and your company.

The next chapter is about uber-networking. Being a super networker and a lot of that has to do with the "after" phase.
Just remember that **following up** can be the make or break of any potential relationship.

If you promised to follow up, to give them a call or even just emailing someone with some information like a book title or website that you were talking about and you don't, you endanger all the work that you have done. You become someone that didn't do what they said they would.

You are less than reliable, someone who broke a trust.

And no one, absolutely no one does business with people they can't count on.

There is a well known axiom of "Giver's Gain". Just remember it doesn't have to be leads, referrals or business. You can give them a great website to help them with their business, a book with tips on how to improve or **even give them something personal** and not business oriented, give. And you <u>will</u> gain.

Quick Tip - You promised to send them information on ...... and you can't find it. Most people would say "Oh well" and then forget about it.
Contact the person and let them know that you looked, "sorry about that, but I can't find it." By doing that, you showed them that you actually made the effort and didn't "just forget". What a thoughtful gesture that would be. A GREAT impression to leave them with!

Chapter 15

Mastering the Follow Up

There is a popular book on network titled "Never Eat Alone" by Keith Ferrazzi. It can be described as the bible of tips and ways to become an uber-networker.

Uber-networkers are the upper tier of super or extreme networking. If you know the book, it's pretty clear that the author Keith Ferrazzi, who tells you how he networks is in a stratosphere all by himself. He actively networks around the clock and throws parties together with the purpose of connecting people together. It's pretty clear that the man not only networks when he's "eating", but also when he's walking, talking and goodness knows what else.

So what can make you an uber-networker?

Two simple (related) things.

The first is to really get to know and remember interesting points of another persons life. Certainly, birthdays, spouses and kids names are pretty minimum. But what does the person do on their spare time? What about quirks? Do they collect ducks or plastic flamingos? How do they vacation? Museums or Beaches? Do they like to read a good trashy novel when they are on the beach or are they worried about skin cancer? There is a thousand bits of information about a person's makeup and interests. The more you know about them, the better you'll understand them.

Now let's not stalk. Going to networking events with a pen and pad of paper, lurking around groups that are talking and jotting down notes would be not only weird, but pretty scary! Think about regular conversations that you have had with people. There are little tidbits constantly being dropped about the persons interests during the course of any conversation as they discuss sports, vacations, business, family life and so on.

Figuring out how you are going to RETAIN that information is something you need to work out.

Again, whipping out a pad and paper and scribbling away or taking out your personal recorder and sticking it in their faces would be a conversation damper to say the least.

Here are some ways that might work for you –
• Create a valid opportunity to write something down. It may be to promise them information or to contact them. If you have their business card, even better. Jot on the back the information "Call Joe tomorrow", but you know can quickly write down that he just celebrated his birthday, rabid Bears fan, is into Hummel figurines, she loves Coach bags and so on.
• You've finished chatting, can you step away and discreetly record some of the information you picked up. An appropriate way is if your cell phone has a recording element to it. So while you're recording those tidbits, it looks like you're just making a call or text yourself a note.
• Go to the bathroom or go outside for a smoke. Jot down the relevant info and head back.
The bottom line to get the information and retain it with tact and discretion. Do what comes naturally.

So now that you have all this personal information, what do you do with it? This is the second thing you do to obtain uber-networkhood. Using what you got.

Some ideas could be to

• Sending a birthday card with a personal note, "Hey Suzy, hope your birthday is a great one". Or " I remember your birthday was around now, can I buy you lunch to celebrate?"
• Emailing Frank about that incredible game last weekend (Frank's favorite team)

- Writing a note to Bob mentioning that you remember he was into Hummel figurines and you happened to see that they were having a show displaying them coming soon. Throw in the clipped article or web link.

- Sending a note to Nancy, "I remember our great conversation at the last event where you were talking about the problems you had motivating your people and I stumbled across this article/website/vendor, so I thought of you and I'm passing it on!"

- "Morning Beth, I remember you saying you liked (author name) books when you go on vacation and I was just at the Barnes & Noble and there is a new one out. Was just wondering if you've seen it".

And so on.

What you are doing is raising the level of the relationship to maybe not friend, but certainly friendly acquaintance that is aware of what they do in their lives (and isn't it nice to know that people show a genuine interest?) and are making an effort to recognize and support that.

But again, it needs to be natural. For example, you don't need to pretend to be a Hummel figurine collector to mention that you saw an upcoming event and thought about Bob and his interest. In that case, you paid attention to their interest and are passing on some info that supports their hobby. If you are not a sports fan, and you're trying to come off as one, it will ring false and be pretty obvious. You can still go up and say "Hey Frank, didn't you say that you are a Notre Dame fan and aren't they doing pretty decent this year?" Shows you listened, but aren't quite following their team. And trust me, the fan will be more than happy to fill you in on all the details.

A quick note on automated processes. We have a lot of business tools available today where you get someone's name and send out cards, messages, newsletters periodically about local happenings, general interest items, etc. This isn't bad.

It <u>does</u> keep your name and your organization in their minds, however don't mistake it for the strength of the personal touch, the "I was thinking of you" action. It's something that can't be automated or faked.

So these are the two things you can do.
1. Understand and collect information about people and their lives.
2. Act on it. It gives you the opportunity to build a relationship that shows you listen, you remember and that you are interested in them and their lives.

By doing that, you are creating an opportunity for a deeper and more significant relationship. You are exhibiting a memorable thoughtfulness. And it naturally flows that they will want to support you in your business and your success.

Think on it. Act on it. Put away time during your week designed expressly for doing follow-up. It's kind of fun and guarantee you will profit from it.

Be honest, supportive and thoughtful in your dealings.

And a new uber-networker will be born!

Chapter 16

Gaining Instant Credibility

Networking is all about building relationships. Building that Like, Trust and Respect where you gain rapport and credibility, so people will want to get to know you and see that you are a person they want to do business with (or just get to know better!).

But there ARE several ways to gain *instant credibility* with people, giving you the opportunity to separate yourself from the herd.

When first meeting people, we put them through a mental obstacle course. We wonder if this person is valid, someone that you could like, trust and respect (mostly trust).

Have you ever been to an event and you are talking with someone when a third party comes up and says, "I've used John's services and he's just great! Yadda-yadda-yadda (the details that is!). Your opinion of that person takes an automatic leap. By getting that "attaboy", credibility in everyone's eyes rises instantaneously and they'll advance a few squares (so to speak) of trusting that this could be a person you could do business with.

Now, I'm not suggesting that you hire a professional plugger for yourself, where they wait until you engage in conversation with someone and then on signal come running up and start proclaiming the wonder of your services. But are you attending networking events with people that have used your services? It certainly wouldn't be out of line, to ask them to mention it or be available if you told someone that "Sue over there has used my services and maybe she'd share with you her thoughts". Instant Credibility! (Just make sure you know what Sue is going to say!)

While writing this I was at a networking event where you sit at a large round table and introduce yourself. As I was giving my commercial, one lady interrupted me and mentioned that she had attended one of my workshops not too long ago.

After asking her how she felt about the workshop, she took up all MY allotted time telling everyone how great it was for her. I'm certainly not complaining since there was absolutely nothing I could have said that would have had a more positive impact than her comments for my workshop that day.

Another way to gain credibility in short order is to be a speaker. Many organizations, especially chambers, associations and networking groups are looking for people to speak to their members on relevant topics. Being a speaker gives you instant credibility as a knowledge expert.
People that don't even attend your engagement will still give you that "expert" status when they find out you did a presentation.
There are pitfalls however and public speaking has a whole bunch of them. The two top pitfalls are you really need to do a decent job speaking and secondly, not be focusing on doing an infomercial. Infomercials, where you basically do a 30 minute sales presentation *where they get 25% off if they sign up today* (there are still people doing this) are a huge turn-off for the vast majority of participants.
Presenting a good, informative talk on topics pertinent to your listeners immediately puts you in front of numerous people allowing you to present yourself as an "expert" that wants to help them improve their life/career/business. And provide a handout with "10 tips" on a sheet of paper that has your contact information.
No hard sell, just instant credibility.
Interested, but petrified at the thought? Check out your local Toastmaster's group to hone your skills.

Another way is to write articles. There are a lot of publications out there, again chamber/neighborhood newsletters come to mind that would like submissions. There are also online venues, such as ezinearticles.com that accept articles. The articles themselves will also be a long term marketing solution to gain business or traffic from.

46

And being able to say in a conversation, "oh, yes, I've published an article on that very subject", immediately alters your status. People who write articles are considered knowledge experts, once again giving you instant credibility.

Bringing the subject up needs to be natural however. If you're running around telling people you write articles may not have much effect (or at least the effect you want). If a topic is being discussed and you casually mention your article. You can expect positive interest in knowing you better. It also may give you the opportunity to follow up with the link to your article!

The last and potentially most rewarding way to gain credibility is to take a position within the organization.
Get on the board, or a committee. If the group has them, become an ambassador greeting new people. If you're networking to meet new people isn't that a great position to be?

Board members, etc. get a certain introductory leap in Like, Trust and Respect. Let's face it, we're impressed and maybe a little flattered when a board member comes up and talks to us.
As a board member, people believe that you are going to be connected whether in the community or the organization and that you are a good person to get to know. Someone they should know. Instant credibility.

QUICK TIP: There can be a pitfall going this route however. You need to be an ACTIVE board member committed to the group/association. I once met a guy at a particular association networking event who had a big VP-MEMBERSHIP name tag. When I mentioned it, his reply was that he just does it for the contacts. Thanks very much, I moved on.

47

Board members ARE likely to be highly connected people within that community. As a fellow board member (that gets things done!) YOU will have upfront and repeated face time which gives you an excellent opportunity to build relationships with those potentially influential and connected people in a very quick time. They will see you in action and when they like what they see, it's all gold from there.

People go through a buying process. It's a well known axiom that they first have to "buy" you; then "buy" your company and then lastly, your product. Remember that Like, Trust and Respect from earlier? One of the great things is that Respect is Respect. If someone respects you for the work on the board (for example) it has a tendency of bridging over to giving you respect and trust on how you perform professionally, even if they've never seen your work. They TRUST that you will be consistent in that area, because they've "seen you in action" in another.

If you are someone who is recommended (first example), knowledge expert (speaking or writing) or an organizational leader, you give people an opportunity to "buy you" without the normal "vetting" process. You gain an instant credibility of being someone **they** want get to know better. And wouldn't that be a great position to be in when you network?

Chapter 17

Closing Up

Ok, here's the deal. I've loaded you with a ton of information.

Adjust the idea of how networking can benefit you...it's not <u>all</u> about finding more clients. Now you should have a clearer idea of what exactly is involved when we talk about relationships.

Learn to do a little prep work prior to going to any networking event. Get your head in the right place, target some people that can be resources and set some goals of what you want to accomplish.

Always be yourself, but be professional. Get rid of behaviors or appearances that put road blocks in your way. Treat people with interest and respect, even if you don't see where they fit in to your present situation. It doesn't cost you anything and you don't know what's around the corner. They may not be a resource or client today, but there is always tomorrow, or the day after!

Learn to listen well and instead of trying to show how smart you are when you speak, **figure out a way to show them how smart they are**. If you can do that, you'll be a person that they will want a relationship with.

Don't forget basic courtesy or following up. The fact is that these things are not widely done and will mark you as someone different in a refreshingly positive way. When you follow up, you show that you are someone that they can count on. Always a (big) point in your favor.

Strive to be better, to improve. Good networkers are rare. If you give a damn when you network, show professionalism, interest and responsibility, it will resonate with those you meet.

Networking where ever you do it, socially, personally, professionally should be worth your time, enjoyable and rewarding.

Networking is all about relationships, you helping people, people helping you, connecting in ways that you may not initially foresee.

Focusing on HOW to network better is what this book has been about. I sincerely hope you have found points that will help you be a more successful networker.

Use the worksheet in the following page to create some networking goals and write some ways that you can be a more effective networker. It will be worth your trouble.

You now have the tools, so the time to begin exploring is now.

Networking Worksheet

Some Goals That Would Be Good For Me To Have -

Jot down several Goals that make sense for You/your Business

_____

_____

_____

_____

_____

Areas That I Can Work On-

Choose several things that you can do to make your networking more effective. After listing, create a priority for which ones you'll focus on first and give yourself a target date of when you'll try to put it into action.

Goal	Priority	Target Date

About the Author

Terry Bass is a business coach who speaks, presents dynamic and engaging webinars, seminars and workshops, along with some of the most empowering development programs being offered today.

While he lives in the ChicagoLand (IL) area, Terry's presentations and workshops have been seen nationwide.

The author uses his extensive coaching, training and business background to work with individuals and businesses to help them excel in today's business environment.

Terry's last position in the corporate world was National Training Manager of Tech Services Intl. (a subsidiary of Eastman Kodak) where his career involved supporting people, providing solutions and creating exceptional customer service.

As a business coach, Terry gets most of his work through meeting people face to face, meaning networking of course. Besides reading some great books and articles, Terry observed and developed what was effective and not so effective when he networked.

One of his most popular presentations/workshops continues to be on Business Networking where he presents audiences with insightful and real world experiences and some humorous blunders too!

Terry brings his energy and enthusiasm to a range of today's business topics and challenges engaging his audience in a dynamic way.

More on Terry and his company can be found at www.chadons.com.

Credits

Thanks to –

Never Eat Alone ..Keith Ferrazzi
THE book on being the consummate networker!

What Got You Here, Won't Get You There ..Marshall Goldsmith
 More a behavior change book, but great sections dealing with communication.

Non-Stop Networking ..Andrea Nierenberg

Networking for Dummies
Good solid basics for the beginning networker

If you go to Amazon.com and search for business networking books, they will come up with slightly under a gazillion hits. Knowing that they are talking about the hardback version, the paperback version, the revised version, it's still a LOT of networking books.
IF you practice the skills from my book and still feel that you are coming up short, certainly have at it. And drop me a line if you run into something profound!

Some business Networking Organizations

BNI or Le Tip *www.bni.com* or *www.letip.com*
These are networking lead referral organizations that allow you to visit them a couple of times to see if they are useful for you.

Your local chamber is usually a great place to network and "get your feet wet".